1 MONTH OF FREE READING

at

www.ForgottenBooks.com

By purchasing this book you are eligible for one month membership to ForgottenBooks.com, giving you unlimited access to our entire collection of over 1,000,000 titles via our web site and mobile apps.

To claim your free month visit:

www.forgottenbooks.com/free1374999

ISBN 978-1-397-31222-8
PIBN 11374999

This book is a reproduction of an important historical work. Forgotten Books uses
state-of-the-art technology to digitally reconstruct the work, preserving the original format
whilst repairing imperfections present in the aged copy. In rare cases, an imperfection in
the original, such as a blemish or missing page, may be replicated in our edition. We do,
however, repair the vast majority of imperfections successfully; any imperfections that
remain are intentionally left to preserve the state of such historical works.

ANNUAL ADDRESS

ON METHODS OF

FOSTERING THE INTERESTS

OF

MEDICAL SCIENCE AND ITS VOTARIES

BY

S. BARUCH, M. D.,

OF CAMDEN, S. C.,

PRESIDENT OF SOUTH CAROLINA MEDICAL
ASSOCIATION, 1873.

CHARLESTON, S. C.:

EDWARD PERRY, PRINTER, STATIONER AND BOOK BINDER,

149 Meeting Street, Opposite Charleston Hotel.

1874.

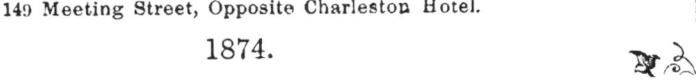

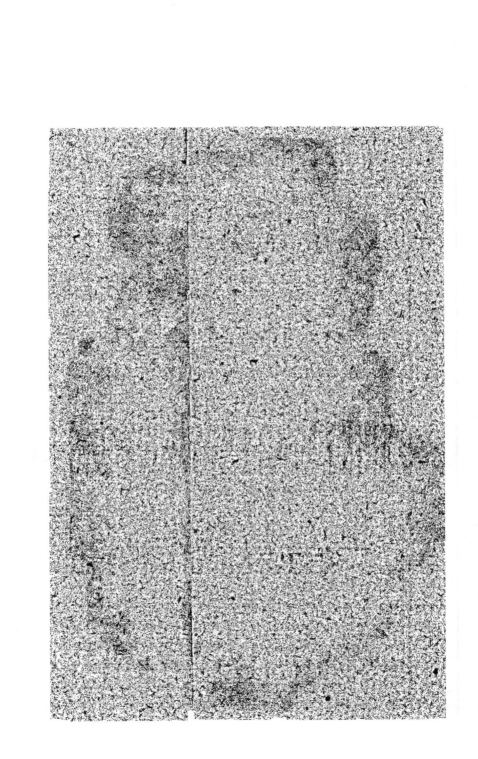

ANNUAL ADDRESS

ON METHODS OF

FOSTERING THE INTERESTS

OF

MEDICAL SCIENCE AND ITS VOTARIES

BY

S. BARUCH, M. D.,

OF CAMDEN, S. C.,

PRESIDENT OF SOUTH CAROLINA MEDICAL
ASSOCIATION, 1873.

CHARLESTON, S. C.:

EDWARD PERRY, PRINTER, STATIONER AND BOOK BINDER,

149 Meeting Street, Opposite Charleston Hotel.

1874.

ANNUAL ADDRESS

ON

Methods of Fostering the Interests of Medical Science and its Votaries—By S. Baruch, M. D., President of South Carolina Medical Association, 1873.

GENTLEMEN : Abandoning your ordinary pursuits, you, the representatives of progressive medicine, in this State, have assembled here to lay your tribute upon the common altar of science.

I extend to you a warm and cordial greeting! In these trying times, when sordid utilitarianism, selfishness, love of gain, and worship of mammon, run riot over the land, and pollute the wellsprings of all that is noble, good and pure—men, who are eager to devote their time and energies to the encouragement of the high aims of this Association—men, who, leaving the imperative demands of their important home duties, gather here, intent upon promoting the interests of their chosen calling—such men are worthy representatives of a profession whose loftiest aspirations have ever been for the welfare of mankind, and whose unselfish sacrifices in the interest of suffering humanity illumine the pages of history, from the time their great master himself offered his illustrious example of patriotism and self-abnegation, to the present day, when numbers lay down their very lives amid the ghastly scenes of pestilence-stricken cities, leaving to us a proud heritage of noble valor and self-denial, which, though unheralded by the historian's pen, will float down into the turbid ocean of base human passions, as the genial gulf stream, infusing warmth and purity into its frigid depths.

For twenty-five years the physicians of this State have annually congregrated, when not interrupted by uncontrollable events, ani-

mated by the same lofty aims that have prompted you to gather
here on this day.

The scientific and literary productions of our predecessors, as recorded in the medical literature of their day, have shed lustre upon
the profession which they adorned, and have contributed to enhance
the fame achieved by other citizens of this commonwealth in the
science, arts, literature, jurisprudence, and statesmanship. The
State that claims a Bachman, a Washington Allston, a Gilmore
Sims, a Petigru, and a Calhoun, may add with just pride her
Holbrook, her Moultrie, her Dickson, her Nott, her Sims, her
Thomas, and Geddings, to the constellation of great names that
adorn her escutcheon. It behooves us, not only to perpetuate the
achievements of those whose mantle has fallen upon us, but it is
incumbent upon us to hew out for our generation a brilliant path-
way through the tangled mazes of scientific research.

I beseech you, gentlemen, to rise from the slough into which the
disasters of war, the wreck of fortunes, and the calamities of bad
government have plunged us. Bearing in mind the humane
spirit of our calling, let us soar above the din and strife of contend-
ing factions, and bend all our energies to restore the high reputation for dignity, learning, and zeal, which the medical profession of
this State has so worthily been accorded in times past.

. Let us take counsel as to the best methods of securing the benefits of individual experience.

Living in an age of vast intellectual force, we are urgently ap-
pealed to, to lend our aid to the elevation of the grand structure of
philosophic medicine, which is now rearing its lofty proportions
amid the tottering ruins of fallacious doctrines—doctrines that are
succumbing to the onslaughts of modern chemistry, physiology and
microscopy, and their resultant, a sound pathology. Let us contribute to the grand fruition of the labors of Virchow, Niemeyer,
Brown-Séquard, Beale, Paget, Rindfleisch, Cohnheim, and others,
whose busy hands and minds are toiling to erect a structure, that
will serve as a beacon-light to our successors, divesting *their* efforts
in behalf of suffering humanity, of that empiricism which forces *us*
often to grope and stumble in obscurity and confusion.

Light! light! is the watchword emblazoned upon the banners of
the present generation! In all departments of research, more light
is anxiously sought. The gentle flame of inquiry is stirred into a

seething blaze by an all-pervading skepticism, which subjects all ideas and propositions, however sacred and time-honored, to its relentless attacks.

Shall we stand idle, while the tide of progress and enlightenment is rushing past us? Let us rather take it at the flood, and freight its heaving bosom with the products of our own hands and minds. Let us not prove recreant to the duty we owe to ourselves, our time and generation, lest, when we are laid in the dust, our names be remembered only with scorn, as idle sluggards, who permitted the golden opportunity to escape.

I ask you, gentlemen, to follow me, while I occupy a portion of your time with a few thoughts upon some of the *methods of fostering the interests of our science, and its votaries.*

Preeminent among these stands the establishment and maintenance of active medical organizations.

A large proportion of the triumphs of modern medicine was achieved by members of medical societies. Stimulated to active research by the attrition of opposing views, and drawing inspiration from congenial minds, many an humble laborer in the field of scientific research has wrought out valuable results. These were presented to the searching test of discussion, and then reached the profession through its literature. As a recent example, I may mention chloral. The record of the first cases in which this hypnotic was administered to the human economy, was presented before the Berlin Medical Society, by Professor Langenbeck. From that moment it was promulgated to the world, and thus Liebreich's great discovery rapidly became the property of physicians, from whom it has since received such high encomiums. But, although we may not number in our midst minds which are destined to revolutionize systems or create new eras in medicine, there is much to be accomplished by organized effort, that may be of no less import in the practical application of existing theories.

The recorded experience of intelligent men is surely of great and incalculable value. Human maladies are so exceedingly complex, and the human mind so variously constituted, that every practitioner who has gathered much experience, and has enjoyed opportunities for much observation, must, of necessity, have had presented to him novel forms or modifications of disease, and must have drawn inferences and instituted modes of practice, differing from those ordinarily in vogue. It is an obligation which devolves upon him, by virtue of his calling, to contribute to the general stock of knowledge such facts and deductions as have resulted from his reasoning on his cases.

The illustrious founder of medicine has well epitomized the value of time and the importance of its proper application in the terse sentence : "Vita brevis, ars longa, occasio praeceps, experimentum periculosum, judicium difficile."

Life is indeed short; it is a dream upon earth. As shadows that float upon the waves, we pass away; we measure our lazy steps by space and time, and find ourselves, ere we realize it, in the midst of eternity. We are now treading the stage of active life, but in a few brief years, yes, moments, our voices may be forever stilled. We, who daily have occasion to realize this truth in our intercourse with the suffering and dying, should engrave it upon our hearts. Is it not our solemn obligation, then, to record here, amidst our peers, the treasures culled and carefully garnered in the storehouse of experience ; is it not our bounden duty to offer these to the test of discussion, to be confirmed as sound deductions and guides for the future? Now, while we are still permitted to uphold our views by personal defence, we must present them, lest, when our voices are hushed, we may be misrepresented by our own facts. Cullen has said : " There are more false facts in medicine than there are false theories."

Let us not be silent, but offer our facts, and defend them while we may.

An Arabian sage has said :

> "What good comes from Alis sword, if it be sheathed ?
> "What good from Sadis tongue, if it be silent ?"

Of what value are all the vast facts gathered at the bedside by every intelligent observer, if they are unrecorded ?

They die with their creator ; they are lost to the world. A science which imperatively appeals to us for this gift, mourns its destruction. We soon pass away—let our recorded experience and judgments live, then, bequeathing to our posterity their benefits and instruction.

Experience is fallacious ; judgment difficult. Our experience, here presented, must, therefore, be sifted and cast into the crucible of truth.

As has been well said by another, medicine is eminently a science and art of experience ; but in no other is the fallacy of mere experience more fully recognized and admitted. Why should the intelligent physician rely upon his unassisted and uncorrected experience, when every day illustrates its fallacy ? If that apparently most simple and uncomplicated phenomenon—the rising, course, and setting of the sun, be one in which our unaided judgment and best organ of sense are led astray, how can we rely upon our unassisted faculties, when we have to observe the complicated and multitudinous phenomena of life ? We should be ever skeptical as to the value of mere experience, but we should seek to acquire that knowledge of principles, (scientia) by which alone experience can be corrected and rendered available to art.

And while we are skeptical as to the results of experience, let us also not be blind to the imperfections of science. Perhaps the phenomena of life can never be so subjected to the dominion of the human intellect, and comprehended so fully by the philosopher as are others in nature, which would first appear more beyond his grasp. It would appear as if a knowledge of the infinitely great and simple in nature, were much more attainable than of the infinitely minute and complicated, and that man is better capable of grasping the illimitable in space and number, than the nature of the smallest and simplest organism. The philosophical physician, therefore, accepts empirical experience in the cure of disease, whenever it is so offered, as to satisfy his judgment that it is not fallacious ; for to defer the adoption of a useful and practical method of healing, until a science, necessarily imperfect, demonstrates its fitness, would be criminal.

We are bound to advance the science as far as lies in our power, but our first duty is to practice the art with the greatest success.

To accomplish the latter, it is meet and necessary that all experiments and observations on health and disease, by whomsoever made, all facts and phenomena of life, likely to shed light upon the science, or add to the art of medicine, nay, all things, whatsoever, relating thereto, should be accorded a calm investigation from the profession.

"Pro humanitate" is the watchword of our calling, and, guided by this pillar of fire, we should not shrink from wandering even through the deserts, in order to gather the manna of health, for those who have entrusted their most precious and sacred possessions—their lives and happiness—into our keeping.

A true and a broad catholicism should pervade our endeavors to render dutiful service to science and humanity ; its benign influence will ameliorate the severity of preconceived notions, and tone down the asperities of bitter prejudice. I would go farther even. It behooves us to cull in *all* fields ; not alone from the beautiful and well arranged parterre of systematic and orthodox medicine, but even from amidst the tangled wilderness and noxious. weeds of those empirical systems, in which some truth is hidden under mysticism and charlatanism. Raise the dark envelop of absurdities and· incongruous dogmas from the writings and practice of the latter, and even here truth will sometimes be found, standing resplendent amidst the débris and rubbish of charlatanism. Human life and health are too valuable to be sacrificed to prejudice, however praiseworthy. Our art must be promoted, regardless of our individual feelings. We should not be repelled by the latter from a calm and deliberate estimate of the so-called systems of these heterodox physicians, who have made such deep inroads upon the minds of a credulous and impressible public. It is but a natural sequence that their dogmas and peculiar dispensations, so loudly heralded by unscrupulous men, should have taken root in the fertile soil of human credulity. If there is any one attribute more striking and peculiar to the whole human race than another, it is the belief and love of the mysterious, which seems instilled into our very being from the earliest moment of our existence, and clings to us with increasing pertinacity, until it is destroyed by that elucidator of all mysteries—death. It exists equally in men of the highest civilization, and in the most untutored savage ; in the skeptic and the believer ; in the poet and the warrior. Bacon acknowledged its existence, and the stern mind of Johnson bent beneath its influence. Even the great Napoleon, the overthrower of ancient monarchies and the subverter of long established prejudices, was swayed by its silent promptings. As Bolingbroke has aptly said : "Whilst plain truth may influence a score of men, mystery will lead millions by the nose." In no department of human knowledge has this propensity for the marvellous and mysterious been more fully developed, than in medicine. Upon this innate principle of the constitution of the human mind, has been built the fabric of vast and astounding empirical sects, in whose ample haven the most depraved imposters and the most unblushing charlatans have found a secure anchorage for their piratical craft, that prey upon the imagination and purses of a suffering public. But, while we realize these facts, and while we deprecate and scorn the practices and tricks of these men, be they humble peasants or learned pedants, it is not the part of wisdom to sneer at the absurdities of their so-called systems, much less attack them with vehemence, lest the quick eye of the public discover a latent jealousy in our apparent zeal for truth.

If, perchance, we should be tempted to decry too zealously the absurdities and incongruities of a Hahnemann, a Priessnitz, a Mesmer, a Thompson, or a Baunscheid, the contemplation of the varions contradictory and peculiar systems presented by the history of *orthodox medicine*, will recall us to a proper appreciation of our standpoint. Among these I will cursorily glance at the most prominent.

The *humoral pathology*, which held sway from the days of Plato, Hippocrates and Galen, had its warm defenders for a long period.

Then followed the chemical school of Sylvius, Wedell, and Dan'l Duncan, who deduced health and disease from a preponderance of acid or alkali in the system. As related to this system, we find the later chemical pathology of C. L. Hoffmann, Pringle, and Baumé.

Themison, the disciple of Asclepiades, of Bithynia, following the corpuscular philosophy of Anaxagoras, held that disease is produced when the basic particles of the body approximate too closely, whereby the pores are obstructed (strictum), or when, on the contrary, the pores too widely diverge, causing relaxation (laxum), or, when both tension and relaxation are present (mixtum). If we replace the term tension by strength, and relaxation by debility, we recognize in this ancient methodician the forerunner of the later doctrines of Brown. This was the dim foreshadowing of Baglivi's solidism, which system was improved by Fredric Hoffmann through the influence of Leibnitz's philosophy. Hoffmann endeavored to elucidate the processes of animal life from the properties of animated materics, *a solidum vivum*. He was sustained by Haller, Robert Whytt, Thomas Willis, and even the great Cullen. The mechanical school originated and sustained by Sanctorius, Bellini, Pitcairn, Keil and

Stephen Haile, regarded the fluids as diseased, the apparatus for their motion as a hydraulic machine, and the solid parts according to their mechanical properties also. They attempted to define their action according to the narrowing or widening of canals, the relation of angles, degrees of continuity, weight, friction and pressure, disregarding those intangible and silent forces in the organic processes, which defied mathematical delineation.

This system had its precursor in Erasistratus, a disciple of Aristotle, who traced the origin of disease to a penetration of fluids into parts where they were foreign. This doctrine of *error loci* was defended by Boerhaave.

Again, we find the nerve pathologists, whose purely dynamic views, seeking only for an inner power, had their warm defender in Van Helmont, who represented his "Archaeus" as a spirit endowed with consciousness, presiding over vital actions. But, especially, Stahl derived all activities of the organism from the soul. According to this eminent writer, the soul formed and preserved the body; upon its influence depended all action and force, and diseases were the consequences of its abnormal movements.

The philosophic Cullen was a supporter of this doctrine. Although he refined it greatly, he did not gainsay the powerful infinence of the soul upon the processes of the organism. He attempted to study the laws of life, and the effects of external influences, with a broader and more philosophic spirit.

Later we note the Brunonian theory, with its sthenia and hypersthenia, stimuli, receptivity, and energy. It was only necessary to ascertain if a patient labored under one or the other type of disease, regardless of those collateral and relative peculiarities of the subject or malady, to adopt a proper method of treatment. Hence this system, relying mainly upon cause, was as fallacious as homœopathy, which is founded upon symptoms. The physiological school of Broussais gained a large adhesion from the profession in France; and the doctrines of Rasori, ably upheld by his followers, Brera, Bonda, and the eloquent Tommasini, enjoyed great éclat in Italy. Both of these were embraced by many eminent men of more recent times. Their doctrines and therapeutical fallacies are still so fresh in the minds of the medical profession, as to require only a reference.

The history of these divergent views and dogmas, originated and defended in the past by the giant intellects of the profession, portrays to us the vastness of the arcana of nature, upon the correct elucidation of whose laws alone, we must base our opinions. It directs us, also, to an appreciation of that liability to error, which is inherent in all exclusive systems. Moreover, it inculcates the lesson of the nece-sity of a calm and unbiased estimate of every subject and fact presented for our judgment, regardless of its source.

From these colossal systems of empiricism, even, which we justly despise and deprecate, valuable lessons may be conned by the unbiased student. To the "médicine expectante" of the homœopaths we are indebted for those observations on the natural history of diseases, from which have been evolved the modern triumphs of therapeutics in pneumonia, the essential fevers, and the exanthemata. The view, long entertained, that as the healthy organism stands under the maternal protection of the laws of nature, so does the diseased, has been confirmed. Those remarkable instances of spontaneous cure, observed under the dietectic and hygienic management of the homœopath, offer ample testimony on this point. How else can we explain those remarkable processes, whereby health results from the chaotic and turbulent forces that violently assail the human economy, and by which the normal springs up from the abnormal, often vivified, beautified, and even endowed with greater strength and adaptability than the original structure? To these laws, too, we trace that vis medicatrix, whose guidance we should ever seek, which arouses the whole organism to rebellion, when it is invaded by noxious agencies, that endanger its integrity. To these laws is to be traced the removal from the body of secretions and abnormal products by an artificial outlet, when they require to be diverted from its penetralia. Disease, we are now taught, is *not* the negative of health, for the same forces which are silently evolved in the normal and peaceful actions of life are arosed from their quietude by unfriendly influences. Order and law reign even where the human eye discerns only labyrinthian confusion and disorderly turmoil. In the apparently discordant manifestations of diseased action, the same guiding thread will be discovered, whose just appreciation will guide us to the goal of success.

Bear with me while I direct your inquiry into still another channel, and draw an illustration of my proposition from that empirical sect, the hydropathists, of whom one of my learned predecesors has wittily said : "The macerated followers of Priessnitz having the fear of physic ludicrously before their eyes, and zealously intent upon drowning their hidden ailments, convert God's image into a veritable water tank, while, to ascertain its greatest capacity, seems to be the full measure of their ambition. Truly, if men were fishes, there might be found somewhat to commend in the routine of these aquatic practioners."

Is the practice of these sectarians really so absurd, that it is unworthy of the study of orthodox physicians? Have we learned nothing from their aqueous ministrations? Shall we profit none from their errors?

Although this school claims as its fundamental principle a single therapeutical measure, theirs is still a system in which remarkable results have been achieved by the influence of pure air, cleanliness, attention to hygienic and dietetic management, and the effect of those intricate and powerful elements—cold, heat, and moisture, to *whose proper appreciation, the therapeusis of the future will yet owe many signal triumphs.*

Shall we stand aloof and deny ourselves the privilege of examining into the numerous processes which have entered into the manipulations of the hydropaths? Rather let us descend from the self-constituted height of pure orthodoxy, which is itself, alas! entangled in errors and fallacies, and examine the properties of cold and heat, as evinced in the various forms of hydropathic manipulation. You will be astounded that so much truth can be unearthed from so much empirical rubbish ; just as *I* was astonished and gratified, when I once succeeded in reducing the temperature of a child suffering from convulsions, in remittent fever, from 106 to 99, in the course of two hours, by the unremitting application of the cold wet sheet.

To this step we are encouraged by the historical fact, that the application of cold water, as a remedy, is an orthodox practice of ancient fame, but has fallen into unmerited neglect, perhaps from the thoughtless opposition of our profession, which, while it justly condemned an empirical sect, consigned a most powerful remedial measure to an oblivion from which it is, as we will see, being rescued by the liberal and catholic spirit which pervades the profession in late years.

It will not be, I trust, time unprofitably spent, if I ask you to trace with me the history of this remedial agent from the records of orthodox medicine.

The Jews, and probably the Egyptians also, recommended cold ablutions very frequently as remedies in chronic skin affections. (The cure of Naaman by a bath in the Jordan, offers an illustration.)

From these, cold bathing was transferred to the Pythagoreans, and it appears to have been used as a hygienic remedy by the most ancient people, as with the old Teutons, according to Julius Cæsar, Tacitus, and Herodianus. The Spartans submerged their newly born infants in a cold bath.

Herodicus, a physician, living prior to the Peloponnesian war, used cold water as a remedy. Melampus cured the insane daughter of Prœtus with hellebore and baths. According to Thucydides, who described the terrible plague of Athens, many delirious patients, who threw themselves into cold water, recovered.

Hippocrates, who recognized the anodyne power of cold, advises in encephalitis cold applications to the shaven scalp, after venesection ; also mentions cold affusions for tetanus. In his aphorisms, he says: " Cold water should be used when hemorrhages occur, or are threatened : it is also useful in the non-ambulatory form of erysipelas, but dangerous in the phlegmonous variety. ' Tumors and pains of the joints, when there are no abscesses, also the podagrous attacks and cramps are relieved by cold affusions ; they destroy pain."

Galen advised fever patients to be plunged into a bath, in the stage of incipiency. Celsus recommends in the pyrexias, cool surroundings, and the application of grape vine leaves dipped in cold water ; he also entertained the bold idea of immersing patients suffering from hydrophobia, in cold water, in order to relieve the terrific thirst and abhorrence of water. This author relates cases of quartan intermittents, that were entirely cured by patients plunging into cold baths during the pyrexia. Cœlius Aurælianus, also, recommends the diligent wrapping of cloths dipped in cold oil around the heads of fever patients; also the application of sponges, dipped in cold water, on the neck and chest.

Augustus, who was a martyr to catarrh and rheumatism, owed his entire restoration to health to the advice of Antonius Musa, to use cold baths. For this successful result, it is related, the Emperor bestowed on this physician, and his confrères and successors, the privilege of wearing a finger ring. The Emperor Severus, also used cold baths, upon the recommendation of Lampridius, and was completely restored from gout. Thus the custom of bathing spread among the Romans as a hygienic and remedial measure, until it reached the height of excess, (as is the case with everything that laymen have learned from physicians.) Vast and expensive baths were arranged, and Roman pride and wealth invented a new source of gratifying its luxurious extravagance, which can only be realized by a perusal of the description of the public baths of Titus, Antoninus, Caracalla, and Diocletian, as rendered by Dr. Bell and other authors. But when, in the middle ages, leprosy and other chronic eruptions, later, also, syphilis, became disseminated over Europe, the custom of public bathing became obsolete, from apprehension of contagion.

In the sixteenth century, Clementinus, Baccius, and Alpinus recommended it again, the latter more especially in putrid fever. In the seventeenth century Heyden published a treaties on the internal and external use of cold water, which created quite a sensation, and received the compliment of translation into many languages. But again, it fell into disuse; the people were prejudiced against it, and the physicians were not disposed to conquer this prejudice, so firmly rooted by fear and ignorance.

In the eighteenth century, numerous writings on the subject were published. In 1702. a curiously written book appeared, under the title of " Psychrolousia," by Sir John Ferrier and Dr. Edward Baynard, who, in the quaint and somewhat vulgar language of the time, enthusiastically defended the remedial power of water, beartily abused its opponents, and sadly deplored its disuse. As Dr. Geo. Cheyne, in his essay on gout, remarks, " bathing made a greater noise upon its first restoration, and nothing could have sunk lower in its reputation since, than cold bathing; and, adds he wisely, it will always happen thus in things fitted to the vulgar capacity, when they are universally prescribed, without distinction and without choice."

Johann Sigmund Hahn urged the application of cold water for the reduction of a high temperature in diseases. But, to two eminent English physicians we owe the establishment of definite rules, deduced from intelligent observations on the temperature of the human body in health and disease. Dr. Wm. Wright, of the Island of Jamaica, and later, Dr. James Currie, of Liverpool, without the mention of whose name a historical sketch of this subject would be incomplete, rescued this valuable remedy from oblivion. In conse· quence of *their* able advocacy, many German and English physicians studied the subject and derived vast benefits from the practice inculcated by these authors. Hufeland, Horn, Reuss, and Anton Froelich, are prominent, especially the latter, who wrote a successful prize essay, which received high encomiums. Drs. King· lake and Good also availed themselves of the antiphlogistic properties of cold water in inflammatory diseases.

In croup it was, in recent times, first used again by Harden, of St. Petersburg, in a fit of desperation, when, seeing his own child on the verge of death. The successful issue of this case, induced Alberle and Hellenburg to follow his example with remarkable results, which have since then been amply confirmed in the practice of many eminent physicians in all countries.

In 1850, Dr. Bell, of Philadelphia, published his classical work on baths, in which he mentions that Thaer treated sixty-eight cases of rubeola, in the autumn of 1825, with only one death, and offers, besides his historical researches, many valuable facts, which aroused the profession to an appreciation of their neglect of the therapeutic uses of baths.

The prejudices of physicians and the public were difficult to uproot. Gradually, however, the application of water in the treatment of disease was reëstablished.

And now a reaction is rapidly gathering, that will place it in the foremost rank among therapeutic measures.

In 1861, Brand, of Berlin, published his first monograph on the treatment of typhus by cold water. Bartels, of Kiel, and Juergensen, of Leipzig, confirmed his views, and re-introduced his practice in 1866. Liebermeister records the reduction of mortality from typhus at the General Hospital of Basle, from 16 per cent. in 1843 to 1864, to 7 per cent. in 1866 to 1870, after the introduction of the cold water treatment. Bartels has cut down the mortality to 3 per cent. by the same treatment. Zdekauer, of St. Petersburg, Gruenewald and Rauchfuss, offer the most astounding success in typhus and typhoid fevers. Dr. Merkel, of Nurenburg, found the mortality reduced from 14 per cent., the average of eleven years, to 4⅛ per cent., besides adding greatly to the comfort of the patient, in which all observers agree.

In England, Dr. H. Weber has been prominent in adopting the German practice of cold immersion. Dr. Theodore Williams used it with gratifying results, for the reduction of the high temperature of phthisis. But Dr. Wilson Fox achieved a triumphant success in the treatment of two cases of acute rheumatism by immersion into cold baths. The patients were rescued from impending death, by the reduction of the highest known temperature of 109 and 110, to a point compatible with the continuance of life. That terrible bugbear, danger from metastasis, received here a telling blow.

In our own country, Jacobi and Neftel, of New York, have contributed valuable and gratifying practical observations in the treatment of low fevers in adults and children, by the uncompromising and unflinching use of cold baths.

Dr. Hiram Corson, of Norristown, Pennsylvania, introduced the intelligent and methodical application of ice and cold water in diphtheria and scarlatina, and offered incontrovertible proof of its vast superiority over the orthodox practice.

I will not refer to other less noted writers on the subject, having said enough to establish the fact that the hydropathic system, absurd as it may seem under the leadership of a Priessnitz, possesses undoubted merit. To regard the system with indifference and scorn, would be criminal; it is the part of wisdom to penetrate beneath the cloak of charlatanism, and search for the golden truth.

I have now, I trust, demonstrated the fitness of the dictum, that "all experiments on health and disease, *by whomsoever made*, deserve a calm investigation."

The essence and nature of disease, its tendencies and manifestations, must be examined from different standpoints; those laws of nature which give it origin, life, and produce its death or subdual, must be discovered, and rightly estimated. Then the systematic arrangement of the data afforded by experience will be crowned with dignity and conclusiveness.

Science, training, practical tact, and an unbiased judgment, are essential to the proper performance of this task. Hence it is of the utmost importance that we should submit our recorded facts, no

matter how well sustained by our judgment, which *may* be fallacious, before the tribunal of professional opinion, for adjudication
as to their merits.

Here, in the arena of friendly discussion, they may be sifted,
canvassed, and examined ; here friendly criticism will deal gently
with our errors of judgment, and wrap the mantle of charity around
our shortcomings, if, perchance, we should have blundered. If our
great and illustrious master, Hippocrates, felt that judgment is
difficult, *we* need not feel diffidence in presenting our views, under
apprehension of possible errors.

I claim that medical societies offer the best field foi the inter-
change of views, the recording of facts, and discussion of theories.
I ask you to bear in mind, that, in fostering the interests of your
organization by prompt attendance, participation in debate, and
contributions of essays, you will in a proportionate measure, further
the progress of medicine.

The younger members of the profession may add their share, by
collecting the literature of subjects offered for discussion, and by
gathering the scattered experience of others, they may thus en-
lighten older and more experienced members, by introducing facts,
deduced from their studies. Among the younger men of the profession, we look for much of the zeal and enthusiasm, which, min-
gled with the ripe experience and calm judgment of their seniors,
forms a perfect whole, from which great results must emanate for
the science and art of medicine.

The social amenities incident to these professional gatherings,
must not be lost sight of in the estimate of advantages of medical
societies. From all sections of the State we gather here, imbued
alike with fraternal regard for each other, and a warm love for our
common calling. Here we may meet our classmates and friends of
yore, in whose agreeable society we may pass hours of pleasant
communion and reminiscences of former scenes. Here we may en-
joy that diversion and relaxation from our exacting duties, which
is so essential to the well-being of the hard worked-physician, who,
of all others, is most negligent of his comfort and health. Here we
may spend a brief vacation, after which we will return to our
duties, better and wiser men, more thoroughly imbued with the
exalted character of our calling, and more alive to the necessity of
study and observation. We will go hence enlightened, more

liberal, and girded with additional strength for our daily battle with disease and death.

In order, however, to fully sustain the efficiency of a central State organization, it is of the utmost importance that auxiliary societies be formed in each County, and that these be diligently upheld. In these local bodies the more immediate interests of the medical men of each section, will find representation and protection. The regulation of fees for instance, is a matter of serious consideration among physicians. There is no profession whose services are more freely rendered, whose duties are more exacting, whose labors more destructive of health and comfort, than that which we have chosen. And yet it is a deplorable fact, that the physician is the worst paid individual in every community. While in all branches of business, numerous individuals are found who have achieved financial success, a rich doctor is a rara avis, the wonder of his fellow-citizens. True, ours is a noble calling, demanding much gratuitous work, which is cheerfully rendered, and offering much compensation, in the knowledge of duty, well and unselfishly performed. But, alas! we are flesh and blood; food and raiment for ourselves and families are, at least, as needful to the doctor as to the other members of the genus homo.

We cannot, therefore, affect to despise the "pursuit of wealth and happiness." It is high time that physicans form themselves into a solemn phalanx, to resist the dangers which threaten them financially. It is meet and proper that they organize themselves into a self-protecting guild, which should present a bold front to the encroachments daily made upon them by an exacting and ungrateful public.

I have a wide circle of acquaintance among the physicians of the interior of this State, and I speak from exact data when I say to you, that a majority of these men find their professional work so unremunerative, that they are forced to seek additional channels to replenish their feeble resources.

Such a course necessarily impairs the usefulness of the physician, it is fatal to a proper performance of his professional duties, and ultimately leads to those disreputable practices, which degrade a high and noble profession, into a despicable trade.

I beg you, gentlemen, from the rural districts, to disenthral yourselves from the slavery into which your own noble impulses, as men and physicians, have cast you, and to face the issue boldly. Form yourselves into county societies; establish a fair and remunerative schedule of fees, and adhere to them with uniformity; preserve inviolate the strict rules of the code of ethics, and spurn, with all your influence, the tricks of trade, resorted to by some men to obtain a cliency. By this method you will not only obtain your just rights and reap the fruits of your labors, but you will uphold the dignity of the profession and disabuse the public of many absurd notions and prejudices. You will agree with me that such a consummation can only be attained by united action in the county societies.

Aside from these advantages, there are others accruing from the occasional meetings of such organizations. Personal animosities will be allayed, the *entente cordiale* will be preserved, and those minor differences, which necessarily arise among men engaged in the same pursuit, may be amicably adjusted. There will be no cause for rankling hatred or green-eyed jealousy, to destroy the peace and happiness of the members, but "as brethren you will dwell together."

I will not consume your valuable time with more than this sketch of one method by which *the progress of medicine and the interests of its votaries* may be aided. It will, I trust, commend itself to every reflecting mind with sufficient force to demand immediate action.

A second method, possessing special merit in its adaptability for the furtherance of progressive medicine, will now engage our attention. I refer to the encouragement of medical literature. More especially would I commend to you the support of medical periodicals by subscription and contribution. These works present a vast field for the development and diffusion of knowledge. They lay before their readers the results of investigations and experiments fresh from the master minds of the age, and they present a mirror of the existing state of the science from day to day.

The progressive character of our science, and of those collateral branches, which have received such a vast impulse in late years, demands that medical men be constantly on the alert, in order to keep abreast of their rapid advance.

There is no method of accomplishing this important end that suggests itself to my mind, as more efficient than the perusal of medical journals. These publications are the laborious results of the most active minds of the profession at home and abroad. Since the day of the unfortunate Nicolas de Blegny, who published the first medical journal, (a monthly yclept Zodiacus Medico-Gallicus,) in 1680, up to the present more enlightened period, there have been few men who have received less credit for their untiring zeal and watchful care of the interests of the profession, than medical journalists. Standing constantly upon the watchtower of observation, these men introduce to physicians, whose absorption in the active duties of practice precludes the pursuit of the inexhaustible field of medical literature, such rich mines of knowledge, as prove of incalculable benefit in their daily ministrations. The task of an editor of a medical journal is, it appears to me, one of great delicacy and difficulty, requiring for its successful accomplishment, thorough medical training, literary ability, a catholic spirit. and a judgment of the highest order. His powerful pen toils for the progress and enlightenment of the profession, for the elevation of its status, for the protection of its interests, for the cause of education. All subjects germain to our calling, come within the scope of his watchful eye, and receive the consideration they demand. Do we not owe these men some acknowledgment for the numerous benefits they confer upon us? Is it not our duty to sustain them in their noble work, often performed without hope of adequate reward? As for myself, I can never be unmindful of the debt of gratitude I owe them. I am free to confess that, next to the thorough training received at the hand of my teachers, I am indebted to my fondness for medical journals for a large proportion of what measure of success has fallen to my lot. I will mention only a few of the numerous important discoveries that were heralded by medical journals a considerable time before they were offered in the form of treatises to the medical public.

Marion Sims' operation for vesico-vaginal fistulæ, Lister's antiseptic treatment of wounds, Simpson's acupressure, Spencer Wells' magnificent triumphs in ovariotomy, and now skin grafting, Dieulafoy's aspirateur, and Esmarch's bloodless method of operating; the numerous advances in pathology and treatment of disease, in operative procedures, and other important subjects, as announced in the lectures of eminent teachers; all these have reached us rapidly through the instrumentality of medical journals. He who eagerly seeks in the latter for the most recent intelligence in the science and art of medicine, is surely a far more efficient practitioner, and a more reliable guide to those in quest of health, than he who awaits the appearance of a formal treatise on every discovery. How gratifying to the physician, whose daily observation inculcates the feebleness of his resources, is the reflection that he is at least abreast of the great phalanx of improvement, that is pressing onward to the goal of success! I could relate to you numerous instances, to illustrate the vast benefits which I have derived from the early information of improvements in instruments, or advances in treatment, conveyed to me by medical periodicals. But I will forbear. Every diligent reader of these publications will bear me witness, that I have not exaggerated their advantages. Let me, therefore, urge upon you to encourage them by every means in your power, not alone by subscriptions, but also by contributions. It is a deplorable fact that so few medical men are contributors to the medical press. Among the sixty thousand physicians of the United States, there is scarcely a sufficient number of writers to furnish our medical periodicals with original matter And yet how vast, how almost illimitable is the field from which physicians may gather material for such contributions.

To follow the example of that vast army of faithful workers, who, from the early period of our history to the present day, have nobly striven to place our science and art upon a firm and reliable basis, is a solemn and imperative obligation. Let us, then, emulate the deeds of those industrious and intelligent men, to whose pens we owe that vast colossus of knowledge, which has established for us, of the present generation, many guides and beacons that will illumine our paths, and enable us to steer clear of the shoals and quicksands upon which the efforts of our less fortunate predecessors were defeated. As I have said with reference to medical societies, the priceless treasures of experience. gathered by every intelligent physician at the bedside, should not be buried in oblivion. Rather let them be recorded in the medical publications of the day, and live, to secure for us the gratitude and respect of our successors.

Such publications would always be received with favor by our co-laborers, although they may not contribute striking and original observations or modes of practice, worthy of adoption, still some valuable results may always be gathered, that the wisest practitioner may turn to his own and his patient's benefit.

As a third method of promoting the interests of medical science and its votaries, I would commend you to labor for the elevation of the standard of medical education, and to foster medical schools in your midst. I will not dilate upon this subject, which has been the theme of addresses, reports, and discussions innumerable, especially as the cause of medical education will receive the consideration of a committee appointed to report at this meeting. Permit me only, gentlemen, to urge upon you to leave no stone unturned, to allow no personal consideration to deter you from an active and unflinching support of any measure that may commend itself to your judgment as conducive to the elevation of medical education. Choose a happy mean between the two extreme factions; between that class of physicians who would exact from the student such accomplishments and qualifications as can only be obtained at great expense and after a long course of training in classical and scientific studies, and that other faction which would open wide the gates of medical knowledge to all who may seek admittance, regardless of adequate preparation for such studies.

And now, gentlemen, what have we, the physicians of this State, accomplished during the past five years of our regenerated existence, to entitle us to the credit of having promoted the interests of our science and its votaries? My heart beats high with pride and gratitude, when I contemplate our past labors.

We have reëstablished upon a firm, and, I trust, imperishable basis, the South Carolina Medical Association. Let our published transactions bear witness, if we have been idle. They speak their own encomiums, and need not the advocacy of one who prizes them highly. Our active membership is yearly increasing, and before us now lies a path of usefulness that we will not tread in vain.

There is, secondly, now published in our midst a live medical journal, which, regenerated by the active and indefatigable gentlemen, who are well fitted for the task, has entered upon a prosperous and well merited successful career. Let us not fail to uphold this publication, which adds to our professional and moral strength in the State.

Our medical school, too, that alma mater which has nurtured and reared many of us, has struggled back into existence, and now displays vigor in her lusty old age. Paralyzed by the ravages of the war, its supporters almost despaired of its reëstablishment. But, thanks to the industrious, faithful, and self-sacrificing gentlemen of the faculty, their efforts have been crowned with success. Without reward, and without appreciation, they have labored for this cause, and to-day the medical profession of this State owe them a grateful acknowledgement for the revival of a school in which we have ever felt a deep interest. This school, which has been in existence fifty years, has taught upwards of 7,000 students, and graduated upwards of 1,800 physicians, among whom many have attained to the highest places in the profession at home and abroad, enlists our warmest sympathy, and is surely worthy of our encouragement. Let it not perish! Rather uphold the faculty by material and moral support.

I congratulate you upon these three contributions of the physicians of this State to the *promotion of the interests of the science and its votaries !*

Gentlemen, would that I might now conclude, but such is not my privilege. I must bear sad tidings to you to-day—tidings that, perhaps, have already struck deeply the chords of your sympathy, and made them vibrate in sadness and sorrow.

Death has been in our midst!

His unrelenting talons have seized upon two of our number, whom we can ill afford to lose, the one full of years and honors, the other in the bright and hopeful noonday of life.

Professor M. LaBorde, by whose election to honorary membership, this Association has honored itself, died on the 9th of November, 1873.

Well do I remember his genial countenance, when, on the occasion of our first meeting, at Columbia, the medical gentlemen of this city opened their hearts to us with such a welcome as will ever be gratefully remembered by those who partook of their generous hospitality. Although actively engaged in another pursuit, in which his great usefulness is testified to by hundreds of the good and true and learned of this old Commonwealth, he had never forsworn his fealty to the profession of his early choice. By word and deed he encouraged the effort to render the second meeting of this Association pleasant, harmonious, and successful. We now gratefully drop a tear to his memory, trusting to others, whose good fortune it has been to know him more intimately, to portray to us his pure and noble character for our emulation.

Thomas P. Mikell, the thorough physician, the genial, the warm-hearted friend, the trusty counsellor, the pure, and upright man—he, too, is gone! What a loss is ours! At the first moment of our reorganization he came to our rescue, and at every meeting he actively promoted the interests and welfare of this Association. His parliamentary knowledge was invaluable to us in our earlier deliberations, and his recent labors as Chairman of an important Committee were only cut short by death. To meet such a man at our annual reunions was one of my chiefest pleasures. Frequent association with him has intensified my conviction of the benevolent qualities of his heart, and the excellence of his character as a faithful and conscientious physician. I know that you will cherish his memory, as I do, in grateful acknowledgment of his invaluable services to this Aseociation, as well as in admiration of his high and generous traits as a gentleman and physician.

And now, gentlemen, permit me in conclusion to offer you an expression of my sincere gratitude for the high and unmerited honor you have bestowed upon me, and to extend to you my best wishes for a pleasant, successful and instructive session.